I0749320

Love and Dread

LOVE AND DREAD

Poems by

Rachel Hadas

Measure Press
Evansville, Indiana

Printed in the United States of America
First Edition

The text of this book is composed in Baskerville.
Composition by R.G.
Manufacturing by Ingram.

Hadas, Rachel
Love and Dread / by Rachel Hadas — 1st ed.

ISBN-13: 978-1-939574-32-9
ISBN-10: 1-939574-32-3
Library of Congress Control Number: 2021931660

Measure Press
526 S. Lincoln Park Dr.
Evansville, IN 47714
http://www.measurepress.com/measure/

Acknowledgements

Grateful acknowledgement is made to the periodicals in which these poems appeared, sometimes in different forms or with different titles:

Bosque, "Hotel Bella Venezia"
First Things, "In the Gloom, the Gold," "New City"
Hopkins Review, "The Bridal Door," "Sleeping Late"
Hudson Review, "Blue Flower"
Literary Matters, "Stars Shine in the Window," "Heart-Shaped Stone"
The New Criterion, "Apple Bough," "Smoke," "Fire Pit"
The New Yorker, "A Poultice," "Love and Dread"
Plume, "Rose-Scented Lotion," "The Moralist and the Colorist," "Cento for the Turn of the Year"
Poem City, "Clean White Shirt"
Pulse, "Horns"
Raritan, "Mud Season on Route 2B," "A Bride-to-Be"
Scoundreltime, "Here"
Southwest Review, "Midair"
Times Literary Supplement, "Into the Wind," "B and D"
Women's Voices for Change, "Tangerine Orchids"

Other Books by Rachel Hadas

POETRY

Poems for Camilla
Questions in the Vestibule
The Golden Road
The Ache of Appetite
The River of Forgetfulness
Laws
Indelible
Halfway Down the Hall
The Empty Bed
Mirrors of Astonishment
Pass It On
A Son from Sleep
Slow Transparency
Starting from Troy

PROSE

Piece by Piece
Talking to the Dead
Strange Relation
Classics
Merrill, Cavafy, Poems, and Dreams
The Double Legacy
Living in Time
Form, Cycle, Infinity: Landscape Imagery in the Poetry of Robert Frost and George Seferis

TRANSLATIONS

The Iphigenia Plays of Euripides
The Helen of Euripides
The Oedipus of Seneca
Other Worlds Than This

EDITED ANTHOLOGIES

The Waiting Room Reader II
The Greek Poets: from Homer to the Present
Unending Dialogue: Voices from an AIDS Poetry Workshop

For Shalom

CONTENTS

Love and Dread

Many readers will have first met the title poem of Rachel Hadas' twenty-third poetry collection, *Love and Dread,* in the November 18, 2019 issue of the *New Yorker*, a few months before the world found itself in the grips of a deadly pandemic, and as country after country went into varying degrees of lockdown, people sequestering themselves in quarantine, isolated and socially distant, families reduced to their nucleus. Poetry has a way of being prescient. Eerily, "Love and Dread" seems to speak already to that world of closeness and anxiety, with its beginning in hyper-focus ("A desiccated daffodil. / A pigeon cooing on the sill."), and the ripples of rhyme dilating to existential "birth"/"earth"; "bed"/"dread" only a few lines later. Many poems in this volume unfold in bedrooms or at the doorway to bridal chambers, the bed the stage for birth, love, and death, and for the dream-world of napping and waking in between.

It is a book about the blessings and serendipity of a late-found love, about coupledom and the fear of uncoupling (the "love" and "dread" of the title), the way that happiness always enters the world with a shadow, that there is something rather than nothing to lose. And form follows function: while there are free verse, quatrains, and blank verse poems in the mix, even a sonnet and a cento, I think the indicative mood of this volume is the couplet, the wedding of opposites, as if translated from a language where "love" and "dread" do in fact rhyme. Hadas' couplets (often in brisk, Marvell-ous tetrameters) move swiftly and spontaneously, while the rhyme also has the feeling of inevitability: “depend” rhymes with “end,” “aroma” with “sarcoma.” Among the poems in these nimble couplets are “Here,” “The Story of the Storm,” “In the Anxiety Hotel,” “Shouldering,” and “A Poultice.” The poem that breaks this expectation, branching out from couplets to tercets, at first as a stanzaic gesture, but finally with a triple chime, is, naturally, “New Math,” where the “I” and the “you” of the couple becomes the “we,” the “fresh entity” of relationship.

Although a new urgency (the catch in the throat of serendipitous happiness) has entered Hadas' recent work, longtime readers will recognize her voice, the way she is unapologetically a reader as well as a writer, a professor who can discuss syntax while tackling terrorism (“patient parataxis,/ my teacher Robert Fagles used to say, / not hypotaxis”), dropping casual allusions to Catullus (quoted in Latin) or Virginia Woolf or Aristophanes or James Merrill. A poem about apples in Vermont quite naturally winks at Sappho. “March Dawn” even gives us Merrill's childhood address: “18 West 11th Street” that was “bombed by Weathermen,/ spring 1970.” Few poets are as good at being conversational (there can be an almost Frank O'Hara elevation of the quotidian), only to pivot onto a searingly memorable line. Sometimes she seems to do all of these things at once, as when she concludes a poem by quoting and transforming Frost: “Home is the place.” Some lines that leap directly into the memory include “The city is a garden and a grave,” or “Neither could the darkness be denied,” or, of a soon-to-be-married bride cum doctor Hadas meets at city hall, “Her specialty was pain."

Although poems of love and of dread braid throughout the book, and often both are indeed married in a single poem, the "dread" poems can be uncanny. One of the creepiest is surely "The Poetry Reading Ended Early," which gives away its conclusion in the title. Any attender of poetry readings will tell you that only a truly momentous news event would curtail an open mic.

Hadas does manage, though, to marry love and dread, to leaven anxiety for the future (not just the personal future, but the planetary one: "The world is heating up" she reminds us) with fierce joy. Dread says that things will end (and not well), but Love says, "but not yet," and inhabits a vast Now. The present says, "fill what is empty, empty what is full." Mid-book we arrive at the poem, "Midair," a poem notable even in a candid collection for its vulnerable nakedness. "I feel the need to hug myself / to block the news that after thirty, forty years, / one partner suddenly can disappear. / Can. Does." "We found each other late," she says, but the poem does what life, what time, cannot, and presses pause. It ends miraculously on an ending that doesn't: "the rescue in midair, where we still are."

— A.E. Stallings

Into the Wind

We hesitated only for a heartbeat;
stepped into a hot wind
that blew us to an unknown shore
where we shrugged off our heavy coats
and turned to one another in the light
of dawn. Or was it sunset? And who cared?

This was nowhere we had planned to go,
but the wind blew us there,
lofted by a force without a name.

Then an opposing blast —
the other wind, the anti-wind, the cold one —
made us put our coats back on
and cup ourselves together, huddling in
tight against frigidity, but still
just enough unbuttoned to admit
the icy draft of separation.

What can be taken away?
This and this and this.
A better question:
What cannot be taken away?

Keep on divesting:
there always seems to be a bit left over,
hot wind, cold wind,
and the long soughing in between.

Blue Flower

The small blue flower I stopped and stooped to pick
on the way back from my morning walk
was called — what? I forgot.
Not cornflower, morning glory, or bluebell.
I knew its modest blossom and sweet smell
perfectly well;
had often seen it
in some such cool damp spot
low to the ground and easy to walk past,
but in another state. Another life.
Hoping it would declare
itself in time, my mind
would peel a layer of cloud or blankness off,
I carried one sprig home.

I didn't like not remembering its name.
The cool pale morning felt a little strange
in the wake of such a year of change:
love, transition, illness, patience,
more joy and sorrow stirred into our cup
than we could have thought.
Our cup full to the brim.
I didn't want to spill a single drop.
Later that day the name
came back: Forget-Me-Not.

Breathing Invisibilities

In what used to be a vegetable garden
but this year is a wilderness of perennials,
a garter snake pours itself into a clump of bee balm.
The tail end vanishes. What else to see?
Breathing invisibilities.
Eyes behind the trees.
Deer bear cougar fox coyote fisher cat
(raccoons and skunks and chipmunks are less shy):
breathing invisibilities. The trees themselves —
that stand of maples networked
by plastic capillaries
to catch the sap in season —
how is it that I never sensed before
their strong roots probing downward,
their branches yearning up
through goldenrod and brambles toward the sky?
Their spines, poise, courage, trust,
those long ardent arms?
Where was I all those years?
Limited to the scrim of what I saw.
Now carrying home a fraction of the hillside's
bounty, apples, berries,
and freighted with the double cargo life
gifts us with if we're lucky,
I look at what is watching me behind
the leaf screen; try to pay
attention to the golden afternoon,
the rustle of a snake

all but inaudible through pregnant silence.
Breathing invisibilities:
whose were those eyes? What was the thrumming music
behind the trees? The train
barreling through the tunnel toward light
again. Dream myth narration archetype
allegory pilgrimage
frozen section: stop. Anatomize.
Go with a burst of music.
Fireworks. Again. Again.
Stop: the light of joy
exploding onto the dark.

The Dance

We think these things don't happen, but they do.
Stronger sun; days longer; shadow on snow.
In a dawn dream I race from room to room.
A ceremony happens in each one.
We think a threshold looms, and then we step
over it into another chamber
slyly disguised as one we knew already.
Do not believe it.`Here we are. I wake
each morning to the blessing of your presence.
This braided bond, contingency and chance,
now loose, now tight, the net of circumstance,
coins and cowries fallen into a shape,
a lock, a key, and one step through the door:
such things should never happen anymore.
We almost passed each other in the threshold,
all but brushed by each other in the dance.
Rosy fingers: moonlight on the snow
or morning at the window? Hard to know.
Silver arrow speeding through the blue:
such things no longer happen. But they do.
Nights and days are mantled by the glow
lighting up the rooms we live in now.

Mud Season on Route 2B

Dark ice, snow melt, March sun, blue sky.
Daylight Savings. Wheel of seasons. Birth,
death: people come and go.
Clear out the attic, shed, storage facility.

My son and your daughter step
into the space of reconfigured family
scoured for the future. Brought
down from winter trees by wind and rain,

twigs carpet the old blacktop, Route 2B,
highway that runs downhill.
Swollen brooks, overflowing,
carve out fresh channels.

The water's arrow is diagonal.
Fill what is empty. Empty what is full.

The Bridal Door

I had to have broken a wrist,
I had to have had long surgery on my belly,
my skin had to be in the process of drying out,
most of my life had to have been behind me
for the leaden mantle of elegy to lift,
for the long backwards glance to be deflected.
I'm waking from a nap. Seen from the bed,
the light though the half-opened door
this rainy afternoon
(the day is dark; the days are getting longer)
is rosy: sunset? Dawn?
Getting up now, carefully, not to rouse you
and padding down the hall
toward a belated bowl of lentil soup,
I am astonished all over again.
What to call this passage?
Hourglass, rabbit hole, birth canal,
miraculous convergence,
remotest possibility turned true,
barely contained radiance that floats
and fills me, brimming bowl, tall candle
carefully carried. I tiptoe down the hall.
The bridal door's ajar.

Rose-Scented Lotion

The level of rose-scented lotion daily
lower in its bottle. And because

we are not attempting to fill it,
time slows to a standstill.

The room brims with silence.
Afternoon nap? Not yet afternoon.

Sun neither out nor in.
March takes a breath.

No chasing now, no fleeing.
What were we after? I

forget and then remember.
Remember and forget

what was after us.
However still you stand, it blunders past

only for so long before it finds you.
However fast you run,

you can outrun it only for so long.
This afternoon (now truly after noon)

it too has paused for breath.
No mad pursuit, no struggle to escape.

The bottle of rose-scented lotion
is neither full nor empty.

Old New House

The past looked bleak but busy,
full but empty. How could I have lived there?
I riffled through old journals for a clue.
I flipped the leaves of the book of life.
Books did and didn't tell me. I looked everywhere.
Attic shadows, brightness down below:
through cracks in the floorboards light was welling up.
A dusty window framed a square of rain.
Out of the place of storage, sleep, and rest,
to scoop the emptiness.
The house of joy with nightmares in the basement:
how could I have lived there?
The simple answer is I didn't know you.
The bedroom: black, but moonlight's seeping in.

Apple Bough

A loaded apple bough
brushes against a partly opened window.
It is as if the branch weighed down with fruit
were emerging from the window,
as if the house's fingers
like Daphne's fingers in Bernini's sculpture,
were reaching out and turning into branches.

A man in the room is advancing toward the window:
his room, wall, window, house,
his apple tree, not mine.
We on the outside — are we interlopers,
I and my band of friends,
I and my beloved?

Why do I so desire to pick these apples?
For whom? They aren't mine; I do not even
want them for myself. They are to give,
this rosy fruit, these pentacles, these pawn-
broker's gold globes, or Sappho's bridal apple
twinkling on a high branch out of reach.

Hotel Bella Venezia

A strand of steamy sun has ventured in
to drape across one calf.
Entangled in the sheet,
I'm sprawling half
awake but skirting sleep,

wholly afloat.
The bed is a white boat.
The hotel is a shell
clasping afternoon's
complicated pearl.

The louvers filter sun.
With the economy
proper to poetry,
which knows how to condense
all experience,

this band of heat is a metonymy
for earthly appetite
or Corfu's changing sky,
now dove grey and threatening to rain,
now radiantly clear.

Although it is invisible from where
we lie, the sky seeps in.
You stir in your light sleep
and reach toward me.
I would not be anywhere but here.

Stars Shine in the Window

Light fills and empties hollows every day.
Dawn, dusk. Unstinting generosity.
But when the black is permanent, the night?
Oh death, be kinder than the goodbye thought.

Bright dark rhyming looks: goodbye, hello.
Two transfixed regards that ask and know
and overflow. A wordless history,
a shadow palimpsest of all we saw.

Lesbia's sparrow hopping down a lane
toward black, *modo huc, modo illuc* — pause and go?
Nox est perpetua. It only seemed
the path came to a stop. Then it wound on.

Cinders. Snow. Old craters. Black and white,
hot and cold. Scrubbed clean by desert air,
a citadel, high, red with afternoon,
abandoned now, but people once lived there.

Next morning bathed in light, god's paint box open:
rose-colored boulders strewn as on the moon
keep their balance only for so long,
shadows shifting over each warm rock.

Colors to touch, textures at which to gaze:
your fingertips have eyes, your eyes are fingers.
Here is my right hand. Here is my left.
Here is what I have seen, remembered, known.

Luminous long looks that seek and give.
Dark of the moon so stars shine in the window.
On the last day of the dying year
it was time to go away from there,

the scintillation of desert air,
the chiseled clarity of Joshua Tree
and get to where
we watched a red sun sink into the sea.

Sleeping Late

You left the bedroom without waking me.
Alone in bed
I'm drifting uncommitted, out of time.
No one is waiting for me to wake up,
so I burrow deeper into neutral light.
Volleyball on the beach in Tel Aviv.
Solemn symposiasts. Contractors from the city
make their presentation. They would like to bury
a rusty Cadillac nose down
under the hill among our maple trees.
I say no no no and they're offended
until I mention Andy Goldsworthy:
a wall might work, red leaves, a heap of stones
to be dismantled afterwards, like dreams.

Epiphany: to get a silent person talking,
ask them about their visions.
Epiphany: for the babies in the family,
to plan a future when the poles have melted,
no ice, no birds, no time. Is it still morning
I'm waking to? So lightly dipping back,
wrapped up in love and trouble,
the tangled ribbons of body and of mind,
and finally waking to the blank-faced bald
simplicity Virginia Woolf may have been thinking of
when she wrote about the army of the upright;
then up and out the door into a world
wild and tame, full of precarious promise,
to be dismantled afterwards in dreams.

In the Anxiety Hotel

In the Hotel Anxiety
I lost you and you lost me.

Ignorant where our pathways crossed,
we wandered both alone and lost.

Where was my luggage? You were sleeping
and wouldn't wake. I shook you, weeping.

I had a question, I had more
that needed answers — two, three, four.

I asked someone who should have known.
He slammed the door. You were alone,

roaming red halls that curved. You knocked
at random doors, but all were locked.

I'd gone to bed, but in which room?
The hotel was a catacomb.

In a blank bedroom without you
I felt severed, sliced in two.

How could I lie in bed and read?
My wounded heart would start to bleed.

Aristophanes knew that we
seek our soul mates incessantly,

long to locate our missing part,
the lover who has half our heart.

Love makes us shrink and makes us grow,
makes us quick and makes us slow,

makes us less and makes us more.
Is that you behind the door?

Tired, I shut the door behind me.
You weren't there. You couldn't find me.

Aristophanes with a laugh
said lovers miss their other half.

We're drawn, he hiccupped, to what we lack.
I opened the door. You had come back.

We'd found each other. Stay, oh stay!
Hold me and never go away.

At the Anxiety Hotel
our story lines run parallel.

Sweet dreams you wish me every night.
We kiss and then put out the light.

But many nights we wander from
lobby to corridor, room to room,

and I lose you and you lose me
in the Hotel Anxiety.

Shouldering

The dream bird father sitting on my shoulder
is singing in my ear: *Now that you're older*
than I was when I left the rocky road,
it is your turn to shoulder the load,
answer questions students need to ask.
You are an elder now. You wear the mask
of wisdom. So you tell them
                                        Tell them what?
The song breaks off. In somebody's back seat,
a baby. Whose? More babies on the border.
Terror, desperation, rage. Disorder
of crowded house, tap leaking, family,
students leaning in to question me:
Where should we go now? Tell us what to do.
The road's uphill, and that is all I know,
borrowing, burrowing, stirring the dark stew,
blended broth of night visions and day,
instructions garbled, watchmen standing tall
and menacing at gates along a wall.
Gaps in the rampart: raw red border zone.
Children wake and cry along the line.
The students' questions pound relentlessly.
Dream father, bird of omen, oh tell me —
the lost, the hungry, the abandoned — who
will take care of them? The grownups knew
the answers to these questions. And now
we are grown up, whose job is it to know?
The reassuring elders, where are they?

The dream bird looks at me and hops away.
Always uphill   the steep road   poetry
Scattered syllables still in my ear
when I sit up and the red world is here.

Marble Cake

Swirled with a flickeringly thin old knife
into golden batter,
the streaks and whorls curlicue
to a submerged design.

Fear: less the other side of bliss's coin
than thin lines hidden deep within the sweet
mixture, a secret pattern
coded in dark and light.

We bake the cake
and breathe its fragrance in when it is done
and cut it, and lay bare the black and white
and sit down to eat.

Fire Pit

Gathered, we watched flames
flickering and drawing us together.
It was hard to pull our eyes away.
Without knowing it, we formed a circle,
but many others in the outside ring
pressed us forward till we scorched our toes
and wanted to move back, but they kept pushing.
Marshmallows on a stick?
Of course. They were hungry.
Here, take it — burnt and crispy on the outside,
gooey and sweet and white and cool inside.
Then in a flash it was no longer
about confection or nourishment.
An ember leapt the circle
and caught, and hillsides, grass, and trees caught fire.
The circle opened out and came apart.
We all were running.
But where was there to run to?

Smoke

Smoke from a massive fire was blowing across the river
into the city: lobbies of apartment buildings,
inner rooms of doctors' offices.

The EKG technician said she could smell it,
acrid savor not of wood but metal,
tang of things burning that ought not to burn.

The smoke smell scorched the mood
of people waiting to cross Columbus Circle:
we looked at one another

with shared knowledge that also contained questions.
What kind of bed had each of us climbed out of
less than an hour before?

Love is a burning of things that ought to burn,
that are irresistibly drawn toward a consuming flame —
the merging and melting of what thirsts to merge and melt.

Not that combustion isn't painful.
You cannot go back to what you were before.
There are chemical alterations.

There are invisible scars.
There is a source of heat, a power, a wind.
Smoke freighted the raw January morning.

In the Gloom, the Gold

If our days were honeycombed with cells,
waxy partitions, then the gold could ooze
and spill its gleam and sweetness
as easily as light traverses space.
Are honeycombs so porous, though? Can light
pass through a solid wall? I tried to clear
a passage so that radiance could seep through
and flood the dark compartments.

But even though it shone
(as Ezra Pound reminds us
in one of his best lines)
more brightly juxtaposed against the gloom,
the gold remained contained.
It gleamed, but it was shy of crossing borders.
And on the other side,
neither could the darkness be denied.

Midair

When I hear of the sudden death of a classmate's wife
or my athletic dentist's torn aorta
or an abstemious cousin's lung transplant
buying him not quite seven good years more
(reasonably good years until they weren't),
my first response is shame at how I tilt
not toward pity but instead toward the shabbier side of catharsis.
Terror clutches my heart.
I feel the need to hug myself
to block the news that after thirty, forty years,
one partner suddenly can disappear.
Can. Does.
Those tranquil decades I envisioned
husbands and wives basking in,
sunset horizons of wide marriage skies:
just such years were what I used to envy.
But natural though it is,
it isn't a good idea
to envy other people's
marriages, houses, children, bodies, minds, or time.
It's better, at least simpler, to repine
over our own lost time.
Iris Origo reports that Bernard Berenson in his old age
said that if he were a beggar on a street corner,
he would stretch out his hand to every passer-by,
begging for "More time! More time!"

So was it those abrupt departures,
those precipitous exits with no warning
that spooked me, or was it the diametric opposite of abrupt,
the memory of gradual decline?
Sudden or slow, both kinds of ends boil down
to the same mortal brew,
sweetened by pity, salted by terror.
Both emotions bubble in one stew.
It isn't only you or you or you
whom, as I raise a steaming spoonful to my lips
and shut my eyes,
it isn't only you I recognize.
It is we.
Beloved, it is you and me.

We found each other late.
This unlikely joy
pulled through a needle's eye,
this feast after so many long lean years —
no wonder warnings of mortality
shake me, avid, greedy as I am,
fearful as I am that what we share
will be snatched away just as we reach out our arms to take it.
Will, want, appetite, contingency,
desire, naked need:
a series of daring launches out from a precarious branch of the tree.
Branch of the World Tree.
Then the empty sky. Then blindly
holding out a hand
and against what odds
finding a hand to meet,
the sudden clasp, the electricity,

with recognition —
the rescue in midair, where we still are.

A Bride-to-Be

In a cramped corridor near City Hall
I glimpsed the bride-to-be, her face aflame,
lit like alabaster from within
by anger, passion, terror, pride — oh, all
of the above. I offered no solution.
She overflowed, and I was there to listen.
Her tear-stained cheeks, her fiery hair, her glow —
she was a doctor, I remember now.
Her specialty was pain.

Horns

The bull between whose horns I perch is life.
The bull between whose horns I cling is death.
Tossed on these horns who bleeding dies
or doesn't die but bleeding, hanging on,

rides, and the bull charges through late winter
as through an icy pane and into spring.
Shards shower in its wake.
We need to make a place for the dilemma,

sweep the shards and gather up the pieces,
clear out a space for puzzlement and grief.
I visited the hospital, came home,
tried, failed to sleep, tossed in confusion,

tempted to shake the world awake and beg
   Oh please explain
   in words of one
   syllable life and death

Keep it simple. Doctors, hospitals
I understand. They seem familiar.
But this last mystery — who can make it clear?
I ride between the horns of hope and fear.

Fast in the hold of sleep, my love, you lay.
I turned to you and clutched you anyway.
You didn't wake. It could have been my dream
that buttonholed your rest. Awake again,

I tried to parse things: here the hospital.
Here the bed. Here the raging bull.
Those, syllable by syllable, I spell.
But who ordained the law

that says we may
walk long together, only to let go
finally, move alone
beyond the world? The bull

stamps and steams and charges far ahead.
Having descended from its tossing horns,
I touch the earth in gratitude, and slowly
walk through the green world. But someone's dead.

Love and Dread

A desiccated daffodil.
A pigeon cooing on the sill.
The old cat lives on love and water.
Your mother's balanced by your daughter:
one faces death, one will give birth.
The fulcrum is our life on earth,
beginning, ending in a bed.
We have to marry love and dread.
Dark clouds are roiling in the sky.
The daily drumbeat of the lie,
steady — no, crescendoing.
This premature deceptive spring
forsythia's in bloom already.
The challenge: balance. Keep it steady,
now sniffing daffodils' aroma,
now googling a rare sarcoma.
The ghost cat's weightless on my lap.
My mother's ghost floats through my nap,
as, dearest heart, we lie in bed.
Oh, we must marry love and dread;
must shield our senses from the glare
and clamor of chaos everywhere.
Life bestows gifts past expectation.
It's time to plan a celebration:
dance at the wedding, drink and sing,
certain that summer follows spring,
that new life blossoms from the past.
The baby is the youngest guest.

But just how long can we depend
on a recurrence without end?
Everything changes, even change.
The tapestry of seasons strange-
ly stirs in an uneasy wind
that teases dreamlike through the mind.
I reach for you across the bed.
Oh, how to marry love and dread?

The Moralist and the Colorist

On a Sunday afternoon in late September,
through the honey spill and dapple of the park,
the moralist and the colorist are strolling,
holding hands. Each waves
a free hand toward the sky.

The moralist and the colorist
go to bed together,
inhabit separate dreams. So out of which
tunnel fortress empty house garage,
out of which forest garden barbed-wire jungle

does each awake and turn
first toward the other and then toward the day?
What have they separately
taken in, transformed, and given back?
The world has blessed and wounded each of them.

What is the default music in each mind?
And where and when
can they cross the line from *their* to *our*
city and river, bridge and hazy sky?
Where is the zebra stripe of compromise?

The world is heating up.
The hurricane veers off this time, this shore.
Omens are not answers.
The moralist and the colorist
hold onto one another.

Heart-Shaped Stone

What you see is half of me.
Over the other half
invisible wings are lifting.

I find myself in a crowded little shop
toward which some friends are strolling up a hill
with inconceivable slowness. You're not there.

Perched on a compost heap of artifacts
to stroke or store, to covet or cast off,
I run my fingers over a leopard skin.

The hill is steep. My friends keep not arriving.
Impatient, I reach for my phone
and touch instead inside its little case

a cowrie shell and then a heart-shaped stone.
The cluttered second-hand shop on a lonely hill;
the leopard skin draped over the back of a chair;

the fingered cowrie shell; the heart in stone.
My true love hath my heart and I have his.
What you see is half of me.

Another Bridal Door

May 26, 2018

Ceremonies designate occasions
always anterior to their celebrations.
The day before we learned you would be married,
doors had already opened in my mind:
then door, now door, doors of loss and joy,
and door of vision, after and before.
Tossed papers float out into the air —
scattered, fluttering — and disappear.
Fresh spring breezes waft the past away.
No they don't. My mother is nearby,
and others. All the ancestors are here,
hovering, shimmering in the sunny air,
gathered where the Haw River bends
and the road slows and one chapter ends
exactly as another's opening
this cloudy windy rainy day in spring.
Ceremonies are meant to mark occasions
always anterior to the celebrations.
Thresholds. Doors. Births. Deaths. A wedding too.
Jonathan and Julia, you and you
traveled along separate roads before
you came to understand you were a pair,
a couple with one destination.
We honor you now with this celebration.
Look up. A door is opening in the sky.
Stand still. Hold hands. Go on your blessed way.

Clean White Shirt

In a crowded subway car,
a calm man sits reading.
Even at the end of a long day,
he wears a clean white shirt.
I take heart from that shirt.
Headlines. Counterpoint of dark and light.
How to weave it into any pattern?
I grew up in a household
where politics was never discussed.
The view was supposed to be of something blissful.
But history peers and leers into our waking windows.
Windows? Footholds in a sheer rock wall.
We perch on a narrow ledge.
To hold to hope? To keep the dream in order?
On the sweaty subway, a white shirt.

March Dawn

For Dawn Delbanco

Likelihood, luck, improvisation,
the meet-your-eye-in-the-mirror
epiphany. Spring opens up the sky:
more light, more space. But wait.
Bomb in the airport. Bomb on the subway.
In the market. In the playground.
Brussels. Lahore. No *but.* No *wait. And and:*
patient parataxis,
my teacher Robert Fagles used to say,
not hypotaxis. No subordination.
Homeric syntax was what he had in mind:
this and this and this and this.
Subway and airport and concert hall.
Blood and soft green spring.
Children at play and scattered limbs.
Or parataxis not so patient: life
improbably gifted, clutched
with abject gratitude. Why she, not you?
Why he or they, a horse, a rat, not I?
Trees in the park spread out their blurry fingers,
clutching at what? Warm spell;
this spring is early.
Blossoms on our magnolia ignite
The morning with their murderous five-days' white,
wrote Lowell, with more local dislocations
and threats in mind. Spring fangs.
Spring explosions. Safety?
Improbability of luck and grace,

oh take me home. But where is home, and what?
Home is the place where, when you have to go there,
They have to take you in,
wrote Frost. Presumably a place where strangers
cannot penetrate to do you harm.
Item: March dawn, wrote Merrill,
whose childhood home at 18 West 11th Street
was bombed by Weathermen,
spring 1970. *The siren drowns in choking smoke…*
Shards of a blackened witness still in place.
O deepening spring.
Home at last, you stretch. In a dawn dream
dark fingers reach for you.
Effortlessly one anxiety
fills the space vacated
by its predecessor.
These replacements last as long as life does.
Another hope, another victim,
another death, another birth,
another narrow, blessed, absurd escape.
Eyes in the mirror that you rise to face.
Home is the place.

Here

Where do you put the anger and the fear?
    Hand them over. Here.

What do you do with the uncertainty?
    Pass it to me.

The sadness, the foreboding, all the rest?
    I bare my breast.

The blustering threats, the dark and stormy skies?
    Look into my eyes.

When you cannot take it anymore,
    shut the world's door.

Out of the noise, the chaos, and the heat,
    this retreat.

Out of the windswept plain of loneliness,
    a sheltered place.

When it becomes too much to understand,
    take my hand.

When it hurts too much to live in time,
    come home.

The Story of the Storm

For Julia and Jonathan, May 26, 2018

Rowboat and kayak and canoe,
the river sliding brown and slow.

A shifting cloud door in the sky
opened above your golden day.

Shafts of sunshine came and went;
then rain was pounding on the tent.

The world's washed face began to shine.
Rumble of thunder — a benign

ground bass to the nuptial calm.
This is the story of the storm:

once, twice, three times, the world's wild weather
worked to pull you two together

here to this hill, house, river: home.
Love's readjustments, room by room,

let past and present rearrange
themselves in one mandala: change.

Variations in the flow.
May currents hidden far below

steer you softly round each bend,
no beginning and no end.

Heraclitus's advice:
you can't step in one river twice.

Ripples; a heron's silent flight.
Afternoon deepened into night.

As the festivities in town
(in synch with moonrise) were winding down,

one more cloudburst soaked the groom
and bride as they were rowing home.

Peel off your long white wedding dress.
Peel off your paisley wedding vest.

Turn to each other, man and wife,
after each drenching storm of life.

Marriage gives shelter, dry and warm
from the chaos of the storm.

Angle and ripple, cloud and sun,
rain or moonlight pouring down,

the river sliding brown and slow,
the sky above, the earth below,

and air and fire layer their design
over the story of the storm.

New City

Winter strains toward spring.
A bird is singing in a leafless tree.
The river gleams, the sidewalks glint with ice
or with a hint of possibility.
A blade of sun bisects the afternoon
street. In such a slippery spot I fell,
righted myself, stood up,
and found myself no longer in the winter
but in a city and a season slyly
disguised as ordinary, yet transfigured.
The grime of dailiness was all rinsed clean.
In a leafless tree a bird was singing.

New Math

Out of the place I knew,
I fell into another
world in which I merged with my beloved;

into a world where one and one make two
but two so closely intertwined
they seem more like a single entity —

not he and I, not you and me, but we.
And so we changed, and so we still are growing:
one to two but also two to three.

I'm no mathematician.
But can I make you see
the process? Portal opens into portal,

vista into vista, limitless,
infinitely generous addition.
The full cup keeps on filling.

There's no subtraction.
There is only giving.
One is drawn to one so that makes two;

two intertwine so that makes one again.
But also something new
grows from me and you —

startling emergence, a fresh entity.
One, then two, then one again, then three,
a brand-new being born to you and me.

B and D

Patients check into the hospital.
The baby edges down the birth canal.
Neighbors assemble at the funeral.
B and D cross each other in the hall.

The baby in her blanket
snuffles, stretches, gives a little mew.
On shaky legs, the ancient cat
is trending stiffly toward her favorite chair.

Strange winter with no snow.
January morning, damp and dark:
B and D are walking in the park.
Goodbye. Hello.

They cross each other's paths and turn to go,
but then, acceding to the gentle weather,
shrug and stroll a little way together.
The sky is neutral. Change is in the air.

The cat opens one eye.
She hasn't eaten in a week
but laps at offered water still, and purrs.
Wait, says her bony body. Stroke me. Wait.

The baby opens two
eyes and meets her mother's: double gaze.
Hold me, nurse me, memorize me, see
winter turn to spring and watch me grow.

On their rounds through the city,
B and D have other errands now,
chosen rooms they silently
enter without a key.

The Poetry Reading Ended Early

The claw of history, plucking
like an insistent cat's,
punctured and snagged the scenery
of the inner theater.
The scenery teetered but did not quite fall.

The poetry reading was one theater.
Dream was another.
The first presidential debate was a third.

Argument usurped the evening.
Only a narrow margin was left for poetry.
The reading ended early
so we could all go home and share in private
the public pain of history,
whose claws now clattered on the floor
like an old dog
that listens to raised voices and slumps off.

Once we had all returned to our respective houses,
those voices filled each darkened living room.
Gears grinding, the machinery of doom
went clanking, slow and heavy as an ogre,
down the long winding hallways
of Upper West Side apartments,
tramping back toward each nightmare-ridden bedroom:

imaginary ogre, childhood fear,
yet also all too real,
with the weird power to control the future,
bulldozer, colossus, juggernaut
whose shambling passage raised a fitful
wind in its wake, which shook
an inner theater's scenery again.
Everything trembled.

The claw of history
plucked at the blanket of each sleeping baby,
plucked at the gowns of all the brides-to-be.
The poetry reading ended early.

Cento for the Turn of the Year

Assume nothing. Take a position:
a girl straddling a bicycle after a windstorm.
It was light when I first began to read
and now it is dark.
Forest which one can enter from any country,
a myth is more insistent than a rumor.
I had to rein in the strange, wild energy,
a part of my body I never knew existed —
the floodlit podium, the whipping clouds.
I learned to talk to devils.
We had no idea we hated ourselves that much.
My mind, often a mystery to me,
turns corners while I sleep,
as though my body now is where I remember.
I write to converse with the dead
and pay my respects to the unborn.
The baby is heading down the birth canal,
venturing out alone and then to talk.
When I was young my hope was to put the world together.
Now I want to dismantle it
and examine it piece by piece
and try to match the jagged edges up,
allowing room for asymmetry,
honoring vicissitude and peril.
As if the world were not being perpetually dismantled.
The wind howls. The web trembles.

Can we find the words to forgive ourselves?
The floodlit podium, the chanting crowds.
It was light when I first began to write
and now it is getting dark.

With thanks to Larissa Shmailo, Patricia Clark, Elaine Equi, Dennis Nurkse, and Sally Bliumis-Dunn, fellow Plume *poets, for the use (sometimes, the tweaking) of their luminous lines at the December 11, 2016* Plume *group reading.*

Tangerine Orchids

These flowers unlock a heart I hadn't known
was locked; mend what I didn't know was broken.
That much was broken I did know. But me?
I hadn't dreamed, as some of my friends had,
of bombs and masked intruders,
mute flailings at escape. I had not seen
the double horror happen over and over.
I'd simply tried to live a little. Not
"closure," not "moving on."
Where was there to move to?
October light, the river, and my city:
staying, not moving, seemed to be the theme.
But then if staying means a holding on
to what is gone, there is no staying either.
Each time I pass them, faces pull at me
and I am no exception. Multiply
my little pain by millions — there it is,
the wound, mine too, but wound I had ignored
until these foxy flowers opened it.
Brought into view, the wound began to bleed.
What we can see, we mourn for and rejoice
that we can mourn. Not mourn and then rejoice;
mourn and rejoice at once.

Care Tips, the glossy sheet accompanying these orchids,
advises: "Trim ½ inch or more
from each spray and submerge entire stem, blossoms and all,
in fresh room temperature water."

Have I been cut? These flowers are bathing me
in water not much warmer than room temperature
and salt, not fresh. But tears, however salty,
are sweet. In Homer they all know that. Dickens
in a newly published letter writes
The cultivation of little gardens,
if they be no bigger than graves,
is a great resource and a great reward.
These tangerine orchids are a resource.
The city is a garden and a grave.

A Poultice

Turmeric, rosemary: blend with rum.
Winter is fading, spring will come,

snow will melt and leaves set in.
Rosemary, turmeric: shake in gin.

Turmeric, bourbon, rosemary:
a blue-green bruise leaks toward my eye

(a week ago I bumped my head).
I swab and bathe it. The bruise will fade

faster with this concoction
recommended by my son.

Soak a cloth and wipe the place.
Weapons are poised to fight in space.

Refugees packed in lifeboats drown.
Cyber attacks: the system's down,

an outage no one can repair.
The turmeric has stained my hair.

The pillow smells of alcohol.
Wind and rain and petals fall.

Sunday excursion: Hamilton Grange,
the empty streets subdued and strange,

the widowed house perched in its park.
White petals gleam in the gathering dark.

April this year is cool and slow.
The stain seeps toward my left eyebrow.

Care for the hurt place: soak, swab, wrap.
And then, before I take a nap,

dab the spot with oil of myrrh.
The poultice: patience and desire.

Turmeric, rosemary, and rum:
my love and I are rocked in time.

The motion lulls us, we forget
the bruise, the wound, the doom, the threat.

The Author

Author of many books of poetry, essays, and translation, Rachel Hadas is Board of Governors Professor of English at Rutgers-Newark. *Poems For Camilla* was published by Measure Press in 2018; *Piece By Piece*, selected prose, will be published by Paul Dry Books later this year.

www.ingramcontent.com/pod-product-compliance
Lightning Source LLC
Chambersburg PA
CBHW020300030826
48979CB00026B/1667/J

* 9 7 8 1 9 3 9 5 7 4 3 2 9 *